IMPOSSIBLE CRUSH

Try Not to Confess

DARA LY

Table of Contents

Legal Notice

The author has strived to be as accurate and complete as possible in the creation of this book, notwithstanding the fact that he does not warrant or represent at any time that the contents within are perfectly accurate due to the rapidly changing nature of information transformation.

Although all attempts have been made to verify information provided in this book, the author assumes no responsibility for errors, omissions, or contrary interpretation of the subject matter herein.

Any perceived slights of specific persons, people, or organizations are unintentional.

In practical advice books, like anything else in life, there are no guarantees. Thus, readers are cautioned to rely on their own judgement about their individual circumstances to act accordingly.

This book is not intended for use as a source of professional advice. The readers are advised to seek services of competent professionals in the fields.

Acknowledgements

First of all, I'd like to thank my editor Sovanchanbomey Chith. With your great patience in editing, this book is made possible. We made it, at last. Thank God!

I also want to thank my illustrator Champey Ouk for a beautiful book cover design. Speaking of beauty, I want to express my gratitude towards the model of this book cover Seavmey Khay. Your picture alone can make this book cover ten times better and more beautiful.

I want to thank the proofreaders, including Veasna Ky, Reasey Ly, Deborah Runnath, Mardy Hak, Sophib Soung, Sovannmealdey Pheng, Sreynith Phen (Xing Xing), and Sovann Chum. I'm truly grateful. Thank you for your help.

I want to thank fans of DARA LY Books. Thank you for your support over the years. This new edition is your stories untold to many in real life but unable to escape your author. You own a part of this book.

Last but not least, I'd like to thank *D2D Print* for publishing this book. Thank you for your great service.

Dedicated to DARA LY Books Fans!

About the Author

DARA LY is the graduate from the University of Puthisastra (UP), bachelor degree of English Literature. He's the Chairman of DARA LY Books, a small book publishing group serving the readers on the topics, such as education, inspiration, and entertainment.

As a lifelong reader, he has founded **DARA LY Reading Space** to open the study clubs for the young generation of Cambodia. He is determined to keep his clubs free of charge, as always.

Since September 5, 2016, Dara Ly has published 15 books, all are for teenagers in Cambodia. His goal is simple (and he's silly enough to pursue it). He wants to encourage young Cambodian people to read 50 books a year.

Introduction

Why do you need to read the introduction when you can read the whole book?

Oh, I see. I see. You want to know whether this book is interesting or not, right? Believe me, it's not. It's a joke! Yes, I mean, this book is a joke.

If you've never loved anyone before, this book is a waste of time. I couldn't be more honest than that.

If you're currently in a relationship, try not to read this book. Well, if you do, make sure you read alone. I mean, don't read it in front of your partner.

If you don't want to get mad at your partner, don't read this book. Wait until you're single. AGAIN! Just kidding. No, I'm not. Okay, I'm only kidding!

All joking aside, **Impossible Crush (2nd Edition)** is the new revision of the **Impossible Crush (Fan Edition)**, which was published in 2019. This new edition will give you a glimpse of the issues and problems that you might face in a relationship. Not to mention the funny parts. I'm not sure if they're funny or just plain stupid. You'll be the judge of that. Okay?

Now can we move to the next page already?

Good luck, **My Cool Reader!**

PART 1
WHEN IT'S COMPLICATED
It's Impossible!

1

Am I a Cow to You?
I'm Just Fooling Myself

Thank God, I've found you. From a stranger to a friend. From a friend to a crush. The impossible crush, I should say. But I don't care. I like you, and that's all I know. I'm not sure if you know that, but you don't seem to care much about me. Maybe you know it? Maybe you like me too? Or maybe I'm just a fool!

Perhaps, I'm just fooling myself, believing that you might love me the same way I love you. It is the most exciting feeling, even though it is hard to believe. It is an impossible idea, and yet I am silly enough to believe the unbelievable fantasy, but my obsession with you has overruled my mind and my heart. I can't go back, and you know that, right? The voice inside my head keeps telling me that I should go on. It tries to convince me that you would love me, one day.

Actually, that voice sounds a lot like you. "*Mor. Mor. Mor.*"

He: "*Am I a cow to you?*"

You're not a cow, but you do sound like that when you're singing, right? Don't worry. No matter how you sound, it's still sweet. Sweet like *tea-orange-cat* (lemon tea). Sometimes I wonder if you smell sweet too.

He: "*Are you saying that I smell like a cat?*"

The funny thing about you is that you're dumb and smart at the same time. You're dumb because you take me for granted (*What an idiot!*). You're smart because you're smart. I mean, basically, you're a smart guy. If you're not smart, I wouldn't fall for you this much, and this hard. I fall in love (with you) so hard that it hurts so much, but I don't mind that. All I'm asking from you is a chance! Just give me a chance to prove that it's possible for us to be together. You know? Like two birds flying together forever and...

He: *"Sis, you're dreaming. The only time I see two birds together is when I'm eating fried chicken. Actually, I'm not sure if there're two birds or just two wings. They taste yummy also."*

Yeah, I'm just dreaming and don't want to wake up. I'm just fooling myself. You never love me. You show me that I never have a chance with you. Never did. Never will. Why am I so stupid? Of all the people available in this world, I choose you. I can't believe I love a heartless man who thinks of me as a friend but can't love me anymore than that. I'm an idiot because I usually choose a *stupid person*!

Sometimes I pretend that I don't really like you, but it only gets worse. The more I pretend, the more obvious it becomes. Needless to say, it is obviously clear; you only think of me as a friend.

Anyway, I want you to know that I love you. I always do, and I always will. I will be there for you when you need me. I hope you could change your mind and, one day, tell me that you love me. It's just a dream, maybe, but I won't give up on you. Or else!

Have you ever heard of the song *"If you can't love him, then slap him"*?

2

My Close Friend Friendship

I appreciate that you have been very nice to me, and I couldn't thank you enough. I feel that I am very lucky to have a good friend like you, and I could never ask for a better one. I respect you a lot, and you know that. You're a true friend and a helpful one.

When I am in trouble, you are there and always help me. You never say *no* when I ask. You never complain about my cruelty and coldness towards you. You never shout at me, and I appreciate that, because you know I hate it when people yell at me.

What I'm trying to say is that you are good, my friend. However, you have chosen the wrong person because I am **never** going to be in a relationship with my close friend. **Not the kind of** relationship that you want. As far as I'm concerned, you are that one friend whom **I never want to hurt**. I mean it. I never plan to change anything between us.

I just want to say that your heart belongs to you, not me. I don't want to feel awkward between us. I just want us to be like before. You know? I miss the good old days. There's no secret between you and me. You shared your secret, and I shared mine.

Do you still remember what I told you? "*Friendship is better than relationship.*" Don't be like a sheep, fooled and fed by your own possessive feeling and dependency. I hope you still remember it, my friend. I don't want you to feel bad like this.

You should find a better person. You will find one, I'm sure. You have a good heart, and more so, you are a good person, so the right person will come to you in the future. You might be asking, "*Then why do you reject me?*"

I think you know me better than anyone else. I am heartless, and I have no plan for a relationship, but I wish you could find the right person who can take care of you and love you truthfully. I wish you could find happiness and money. I mean, honey! Oh, if you find money, share some with me. Okay?

3

A Friend or a Girlfriend? Mind & Heart

I like him more than just a friend, but I don't want to be in a relationship with him. I just want to keep him in my mind, but I don't want to ruin the memories that we have had together, mostly good. I fear that things could be worse when we get into a relationship. I could never ever treat him the same way, and I know that for a fact. What should I do?

He is too good, and I am too bad. I screwed up many relationships in the past. At this point, I don't want to risk it again. I don't want to lose him at all. Nevertheless, my heart is saying otherwise.

Even if my commitment to remain single is strong, I still find it hard to resist the excitement whenever I am with him. I've seen his actions, and I could tell that he also likes me even though he tries not to show nor say it. I know he wants to try. We both can understand each other at the level that no couple could unless they have been friends before they get into the relationship.

I am a strange girl, and I don't really know what kind of happiness I want. It is confusing when my mind and my heart are constantly at war against each other. Does it happen to everybody or just me?

If my mind wins the war, I will get upset because it means I would lose him. In contrast, if my heart wins, I will get anxious because I fear that I could hurt him one day. Either way, I still lose, and it's not good.

Why do I have to stop myself from loving someone who is the best one for me? Why should I hide my true feelings? Why can't I tell him that I love him?

He knows that I have anxiety and confusion. He also knows that I need more time to form my thoughts since I have messed up my mind so badly. Meanwhile, I need to make sure my heart is safe as well.

My previous relationship was a disaster, and it killed my hope after my ex left. Since then, I've never hoped anyone would ever come to my life again until I met my friend. He showed me another side of a man. A different one, of course.

When I was down, he was there to cheer me up. He was the only one who listened to me when I needed to talk and cry. He was the only person who believed in me when I had no confidence in myself.

In short, he is the best person in my eyes, but I can't choose him because I'm not the best person for him. Maybe he should find another woman.

See? I'm lying to myself again. To be honest, I'm not sure what to do now. Let alone to decide. To be a friend or a girlfriend?

4

A Boyfriend
Not Just for the Time Being

You want me to find another woman, but I can't do that because, in front of me, I see only one person that I love. I see you. Why do you bring me in if you are going to kick me out? Why do you choose me if you are going to run away? Why do you give me hope if you are going to break my heart?

No matter what happens, I want you to know that you are the bringer of joy, and my life has meaning once again because of you. You are everything to me, and, without you, nothing else seems to matter. Without you, I'm just a lost soul. You bring joy and hope to my life, and nobody else could replace you. I won't go anywhere else without you.

Every moment with you is the most wonderful time I've ever had. Every time I see the smile on your face, my mind becomes crazy. And your eyes! They have stolen my heart. Your voice. It is the sweetest voice I've ever heard.

I want to be your boyfriend, not just a friend. I want to be your man, not just another guy. I want to be with you forever, not just for the time being.

5

A Secret Admirer

Do You Even Know That I Also Exist?

Do you think of me like I think of you? Do you even know that I also exist? Do you know that you actually have a secret admirer? ME!

I don't want to sound creepy, but I do stalk your *Timeline* every single day, and never get tired of it. I have to admit that sometimes it gets me depressed to see you with someone else.

I like you, but I don't have the courage to *Add Friend* because I'm afraid that you wouldn't *Confirm*. You are amazing in many ways. I really wish that you would know that there is a person who secretly admires you. There is someone who sees the good in you. Someone who is willing to be your... (*I don't know who you want me to be.*)

You are an interesting woman. You love nature and your hobby is... (Wait, what is your hobby again please? What did you just say? *"Blocking the person who has a crush on you?"* Oh my God!)

You are very pretty. A beautiful one as I can see. At least, a beautiful girl with the help of photo *editing apps*. But you are so beautiful. Anyway, I love you not because you are beautiful, but... (*Okay, I admit you're cute, and that's what I love about you too.*)

Besides that, you are a hard person to understand. Why are you so mysterious? Your life is so private that it always gets me more curious. It is impossible, for me, to get close to you. It is hopeless, for you are an impossible crush, and I am just an unknown person. By the way, the things that you do or say are just incomprehensible to me, yet you still absorb most of my attention.

However, I want you to know that you are a good person. Please treat yourself better because you deserve better. You have treated yourself badly, as far as I can see.

From now on, please do not let the world determine your destiny. You are the designer of your life, so you should make the decision by yourself. I know you will choose to be happy, right?

Do not let your fear get in your way, and never allow anxiety to gain control over your thoughts. Never ever let anger ruin your peace of mind. And don't be afraid to choose to be happy. Never regret that decision, because that is the right thing to do.

There is no point in negativity, and it is not good to be sad. Thus, you should choose to be positive and dare to be happy. Your life will be better.

And don't forget your admirer. ME!

6

Thank You
Grateful

I'm truly happy to know that you also exist, and I'm very grateful for your kind words.

However, I have never thought that I am that kind of woman. I'm not that amazing like you have said. As I see myself right now, I am just a normal girl and live a simple life.

Thank you so much. I wish you the best of luck.

7

I Know Why
I Know Why It Was Raining

I know why it was raining today. Because you smiled at me. That's why. Oh my God! I couldn't believe you did. You really smiled at me. At first, I thought I was in a dream. Do you know what I was really thinking at that time?

I was thinking that you might be smiling at someone behind me. I looked back, and then I thought to myself, "*Silly! My Oppa is not that crazy. He must never smile at that tree.*"

If I could talk to you now, I would ask you just to be sure. I want to know whether you were really crazy or you were smiling at me. If you know what I mean. Why did you smile at me? Oh my God! Oh my God!

I've never chatted to you. I don't even talk with you outside. Well, I pretend that I don't know who you are. The truth is I've always wanted to talk with you, and I've dreamed of becoming your girlfriend.

(*Sadly, we're from different generations, and I look like a potato.*)

Who would love and accept a potato like me? You're like a god, and I'm just a silly girl. There is no way that my dream can come true. It's too good to be true. You are way too handsome to love a potato like me. I know it's impossible. I hate it when I like you so much.

My close friends often mock me, and I am very embarrassed after telling them about my biggest secret. That secret is you. Moreover, what disturbs me the most is that another classmate who studies with me also has a crush on you. Unfortunately, she is close to you, and she has met you many times. It frightens me already just to think about that. Anyway, *Crush*, I will remember your smile.

By the way, if you don't want the place to be flooded by the heavy rain, please don't just smile at random girls like that. Okay?

You can smile at me, though.

8

Why?

A Heartless Person

If you didn't love me, why did you give me hope? If you never wanted to be with me, why did you allow me to get too close to you? Did you know that it hurt? You should have told me.

I gave all that I had to you, and you destroyed it all mercilessly. You cut my heart into pieces and burned all my happiness. You put me into this dark place and left me no choice. I should have known that earlier. At least, I didn't have to bear the sorrow all alone. Maybe I could have been less optimistic and better prepared for my exit. In fact, I should have stayed away from you.

My hope was given by you and taken away by you too. My heart was warmed by your care but burned to ashes by your hot-cold personality too. My happiness was founded in you, and yet it was absent when you left. Leaving me was an easy thing to do, and perhaps you had no remorse for doing so. You only thought about yourself and never cared about my feelings because you thought that I had no meaning to you. That's why you chose your own way and abandoned me.

Why did you give me hope if you were going to leave me? Why did you do that? Was it delightful to break my heart?

You're a heartless person. I hate you, and I love you at the same time.

9

Nothing Is Absolute Uncaring

Thank you for teaching me a good lesson. You've taught me that *nothing is absolute*. I shall learn this lesson by heart because it takes my heart to fall in love with you, and it breaks my heart to let you go. I shall remember that!

There came a time when my mind was completely silent because my heart had become strangely aggressive and ceaselessly uncontrollable. It appeared more real to me when I actually saw your face, even if I wasn't thinking about you. I realized that I fell in love with you.

Now I have learned that the only true justice in a relationship is unfairness. I love you very much, yet you are careless about me. I give everything to you, but you never bother to give any hope to me. You are very unkind, and it is very unfair. However, there is nothing I can do because nothing can change your mind.

I become your prisoner when you lock me up inside a lonely place. It's pretty scary. Still, I remain positive, and I pray to God that you will change your mind and accept me one day. In contrast, you even become more uncaring.

I couldn't believe you have turned into a person like this. It's shockingly unbelievable. Someone who used to be kind has become heartless and indifferent. Someone who once showed me the beautiful part of the world has turned into a devil. I couldn't believe it.

Anyway, I still want to thank you for a good lesson. I will remember it, and I won't repeat the same mistake. I will never ever love you again because you are very unlovable.

10

Unpromising Relationship Should I Quit?

People say: "*You can't quit. You shouldn't quit.*"

I'm not sure if I can agree with this idea every time. There are countless times when people can or should quit. For example, gambling. Agree?

Speaking of a gamble, a relationship is similar to it, in some ways. One needs to know when to quit and why. I'm considering whether I should quit my relationship or not. I'm not really sure why, but it's really annoying.

My boyfriend doesn't love me. Not enough, I feel. He never shows me that he does. What should I do? Should I quit?

If you have similar experiences, please tell me what I should do. Meanwhile, my family is forcing me to get married. Okay, not forcing. But my mom always asks me when I will get married. What am I supposed to tell her? Who will be my husband? Honestly, I don't have a clue.

At this point, I want to make it clear. I just don't want to keep gambling my future with a man who is not committed enough. I can't rely on his words because they are always changing, and he is always unsure. His actions are even worse.

I'm getting older, and my face is the evidence even though my height is still a kid-kid standard. Maybe I should think about my future. Maybe it's time to let him go. Maybe I should walk away from this unpromising relationship.

Should I tell him or wait till he tells me? God, what should I do?

PART 2
WHEN YOU'RE UNSURE
It's Unlikely!

11

Unappreciated Effort
Am I a Joke to You?

Am I a joke to you? I really don't understand why you have to do that. I thought you might like me too. Then you told me that you were afraid of a relationship. Is this a joke or what? Why do you have to play this game with me?

I rejected every guy because of you. I ignored those who really cared about me because I cared about your presence in my life. I was thinking that you would make me happy. Well, I was wrong. You brought me another heartbreak experience.

I even told everyone that you were my first choice. They thought I was making a mistake, but I didn't listen to them because I believed you. Now you have destroyed my trust again. You just want to play a game with me because you think I am a joke to you. You think it's funny, but you've never thought about the person who may get hurt because of your pathetic game. Please stop it. I'm begging you. Don't try to be a person you don't want to be. Don't try to fool me again.

I have had enough, and I am tired of being a victim of your game. If you want to have your own freedom, don't act like you like me. I'm not going to buy it. I can let you go. In fact, I'm happy to let you go.

Here is my suggestion: *"Please stop doing this to other girls."* I am a girl, and I understand how other girls would feel. They won't like to be in a situation like this. They will hate you if you take them for granted.

12

Unwanted Relationship
Save Your Money

Love is not defined by how beautiful you are. It is not defined by how rich you are either. It is not defined by how tall you are either. Love is not defined by many things that many heartbroken people have tried to describe. To say the least, single people. They all fail to define the definition of love. That's why they fail in a relationship.

The question is: "*How to define love?*"

Siri: "*Dictionary.*"

Love is not always a topic you want to talk about. A relationship is not always your top priority. You have too many things to take care of right now, so it's better to stay away from some problems that a relationship could bring to you. You know that, I know that, but some people don't. They keep coming to you because you have that charm that attracts people, and perhaps even flies.

Oh, okay, you don't attract flies. I see. I see. But you do attract so much attention from so many people, right?

People say, "*The cow poop always attracts the car wheel, and the charming person always attracts the ugly admirers.*"

Okay, nobody really says that. Still, it's kind of true, right? I mean, you are cute and cool, and you really attract so much attention from so many people, but usually they are not your type. (*I don't want to say that they're ugly.*)

People also say: "*A perfect girl is an unlucky one because she can't find the right person whom she can fully accept.*"

See? You're an unlucky girl because you're charming and perfect in many ways. Do you want a piece of advice?

Here is my suggestion: **Save your money, and stop buying skincare products for the time being.**

Stop being charming for the time being. Okay? You should become a little uglier, and probably, your luck would improve a little bit, and hopefully, you could find just the right guy.

Yeah, I know, this is the dumbest idea you've ever heard. What else can I say? I'm ugly, but I'm lucky, more than I can say.

Anyway, I still don't understand why a perfect and smart person like you couldn't find the right person. You have a lot of admirers, I get that, but, at least, there must be a few good guys you like, right?

Oh, I see. Unwarranted promise!

13

Unnoticed

Ignore

I love you, but you love her. I am jealous. Do you know that? I care so much about you, but you never care about me. You only pay attention to her. You make me very disappointed.

When I am sad, I have nobody to talk to. When you are not happy, I am there for you. You text me one message, and I reply to you ten messages because I have so many things to say. Unfortunately, you don't even notice that I also want you to pay attention to me. I love you, and I hate you too. I hate you because you always ignore me. I love you because you ignore me too.

I try so hard that it hurts me every time. My love is unnoticed. You just don't care.

14

Untruthful

Sorry

I was a fool because I thought that you also loved me like I loved you. You never loved me; you only played a game with me because you knew that I was a silly girl. You took me for granted, and I was nothing in your eyes.

To you, I am just an annoying person, and you only want to get rid of me. You never appreciate my presence. Now I know it. I know that I am annoying somebody. I know that he is not happy when I stay.

I will leave, and I shall be gone soon. You won't have to be annoyed like before because nobody will disturb you and your precious life. Nobody will keep asking you about your meal, your work, and your life. Nobody. You will be happy because you won't have to deal with this silly girl anymore. I am very sorry that I always thought you loved me. You never did. I was always wrong about that. I was stupid.

I love you. I still do. You hate me, and I know that. I also know that I only bring you the headache, but never the happiness. In short, I am bad in your eyes.

Now I shall leave, and maybe there is no chance to say goodbye. You don't even wish to say it, so I should not say it. I'll go.

Please take care of yourself when I'm gone because nobody could take care of you like I did. I mean, nobody would put up with you like I did. I wish you good luck.

IMPOSSIBLE CRUSH

You often say that you want me to stay, but I know that it is an untruthful statement. You're just lying. I'm tired of it.

25

15

Unattractive
The Secret

Actually, I have many of your cute pictures, but I choose to post the ugliest ones. Do you know why? Because if I post your *cute* photos, my crush may be interested in you instead of me. I have to keep you away from him, and I need to make sure he is interested in me only. I know him. I know that he's a flirty guy, so I don't want him to know anyone else.

Sometimes I don't want to embarrass you, but, you know, I just want his attention. I need to be creative, and I want to look funny in his eyes. When I'm with you, we both are crazy, and that's the only way I can appear more adorable, at least, for the time being.

He's also a gentleman, but, God, I can't believe most gentlemen don't love a gentle girl like me.

You can pretend to agree that I'm a gentle girl.

But, you know, he just doesn't love... He'll never love a shy and weak person like me. That's why I just need you to play a role as a fool so that I can look cool and charming in his eyes.

He really loves a charming person. I wish I could be more beautiful than this. I wish I could have a nice-looking body like a model. Look at me now; I'm fat and unattractive. He'll never love me if he sees someone else better than me. That's why. That's why I need you to help me.

Do you know the secret of how to be more beautiful in less than one minute? It's easy. No makeup is needed. No need for brand, brand products. If you want to look more beautiful, you just need to stand next to someone who is uglier than you. That's it. You'll look perfectly beautiful. Perfectly!

Among many photos that we have together, I could find only a few ugly photos of yours. Uglier than me, of course. In fact, you're beautiful. Believe me!

I just have to make sure you look uglier than me, at least, for now. By the way, I will not tag you in this post. Okay? I don't want him to know your Facebook account (*User Name*). I can't imagine when my crush has a crush on my friend.

16

Unbelievable Missing You

I'm missing you right now. It's unbelievable. Love is crazy sometimes, but every time love shows up, it always has a way of making us believe something that is utterly unbelievable. Love has a way of pushing us around, and it can convince us to choose someone whom we never thought would be the one. We are so consumed by blindness. Love is blind, as it has been said, but I am more than blind when I get too deep into the fantasy of this thing called love.

I think I love you, but I don't have the courage to tell you. Plus, I don't want to become an opportunist trying to take you away from your previous lover. Your past. I respect your choice.

I will wait until you can move on from your previous relationship. You're my impossible crush, and I'm just another friend, but I'm happy. I just want to be there for you. I just want to be with you.

Somehow, I don't think I am good enough for you right now, either. The way I see it, you are very good, but I am nowhere near the definition of good.

I still hope, though, that you could feel it someday. I wish we could have known each other much earlier than this. I also wish I could have done more for you.

17

Incompatible
That's Who I Am

I've fallen in love with you when I'm not supposed to love anybody. I am too good to be loved and too bad to love again. People love to leave me, and I let them go. I have never been in any relationship that could last longer than one year. I could break your heart; that's what I do. That's who I am, and I don't want you to become another victim.

If you know you could be bad for someone, would you continue loving him? Do you still walk on this road? It's an impossible goal. Do you agree?

Honestly, I don't think we are compatible. You have many things that I don't like, and I like a lot of things that you hate. This alone shows that we are very different already. We're just incompatible!

However, I just want to hear from you. I want you to tell me. If you think I should stop it, I will stop right now, right here. If you want me to stay, I shall stay here and continue to fight against my own fear.

18

Unremovable

Healing My Old Wound

I really want to try again, but I am in the process of healing my old wound. I am afraid of two things, which are my unremovable fears.

First, I am afraid that I might hurt you because I still think about my previous relationship. People say that we can move on if we find someone else better, but I don't think so. I think that moving on does take time. It might take a long time also. In my case, I don't think I could move on this fast. The good memories I have with my ex are just too many to bury, and the bad ones are just too much to bear. They keep coming back to me every time I am alone. I don't understand why he wanted to break up with me. Maybe I was too bad? Not good enough for him? Maybe I cared too much about him? Or maybe he found someone else better than me?

Second, I am afraid that you might hurt me just like what he had done to me. In other words, I am scared of another shocking moment. The moment when someone says, "*We should break up.*"

I just don't trust myself sometimes. To be honest, I no longer believe in relationship stuff. It's too good to be true.

How can I find a good and stable relationship while thinking about my past? It could make things worse for both of us. I don't think we should. I mean, we could not go to the next level. Not too soon.

I suggest we remain friends like this because, at least, it's better than getting hurt again. Don't you think so?

19

Unthinkable

He Is Gone

If you really think so, then I will follow your decision. Still, I want you to know that what has been done is done. Someone who has gone is gone. If you really think that trying to keep someone who wants to leave is an easy thing to do, then you can try it. I can tell you that it ain't gonna work that way. He is gone, and you should let him go. No matter how hard you try, you cannot change the thing that happened. To try changing it is just unthinkable.

Listen, I love you, and I want good things to happen to you. You can stay alone as long as you want, but I don't want you to hurt yourself. When you try to keep those bad memories, they will hurt you. I can't let that happen. I don't want you to suffer any longer because you have suffered enough.

I will be there for you when you need me. Just know that I am waiting for you. I don't want to disturb your healing process. You can have all the time you need, but don't hurt yourself.

Don't allow the past to haunt your present. You only need to set your mind free. I can wait. I will wait. I won't go anywhere. I still stay, and I will fight alongside you.

What matters to me now is your happiness. If you are happy, then I'll be happy too. If you are unhappy, it'll be my job to turn the situation around. Together we can reverse it. If you only give me a chance. If you only give yourself another chance too.

Don't be afraid. Take my hand and jump. *Jump off the bridge?* No.

Leave that saddening place, and jump to a brighter one. Leave your darkening world and come to me. I'll show you a better world. The world only you can rule. The world where you will be crowned queen.

Because you are my queen.

20

Run When Unsure
It's Less Important

I run when people approach me. That's why I'm still single. I like to keep it that way, to be honest. I don't really need anyone to run my life for me, so I just run away when a guy is trying to do so.

To all the women out there, I salute you for being strong and independent. You alone hold the key to your own happiness, and you know that. I also want to remind you that a relationship is not the only thing that you must have. In fact, it's less important than your happiness. You should do what makes you happy even when it means you have to be single for a while, right?

If a relationship, however, can make you happy, give it a try. It's okay. But it's not okay if it breaks your heart and takes away your happiness. Agree? When you know it's bad for you, you run and you run fast.

It's not selfish to love yourself and keep your life as simple as possible. There's no reason to make it more complicated. A simple life is a happy life, right?

It's good to keep the key to yourself. Only you know what makes you happy. To rely on someone else to make your life complete is completely unsafe and inadvisable. By the way, it's just a suggestion, and you don't have to take my word for it. Be that as it may, you can take my suggestion if you want to remain single and free.

Personally, I'm a freedom lover, and I don't need a lover if he takes my freedom away. In other words, I don't like handing my happiness key to someone else. It's just not practical for me.

Still, we all run into a good person once in a while, and that's when we are unsure if we can take a chance or we should run away. We're still afraid of making a hasty decision and would end up with regret.

Regret is a joy-killing thing. It can be unforgettably painful if used in the wrong way. However, regret can be a good reminder also if you use it right.

Enough with my silly philosophy! Now let me tell you my story.

I met this guy who worked as a barista in a coffee shop. He's a nice guy and also good-looking. Tall and slim, he seemed. I hated to stand next to this guy because he made me look like a mushroom, fat and short. We became friends after we saw each other a few times. I didn't usually talk to a stranger, just so you understand, but I was friendly with most of the people who made mocha frappe for me, and that also included him.

One day, another staff member told me that this guy had a crush on me, but I didn't believe her. Not at first. I just ignored it, at that time. Soon enough, I learned that it's true. He confessed to me in the messenger chat, but he hadn't had the chance to finish his confession. I blocked him before he could. I never go to that coffee shop now.

Remember this: **Run when you're unsure!**

PART 3
WHEN GOOD ISN'T ENOUGH
It's Hopeless!

21

Wake Up

A Shaky Relationship

In a relationship which feels less like a relationship, I'm not sure if I should or could maintain my patience. Someday, I suspect, it would run out, if he hasn't run away from me already. Someday, I believe, the inevitable will surely happen. Obviously, all I'm trying to do now is to delay it as much as I can, but it is tiring, to the point where I should quit.

Honestly, I feel like a halfwit for trying to keep a relationship that is very shaky and unpromising. I think I'm an idiot for allowing a guy to fool me over and over again. The way I see it, he doesn't care at all. I'm the only one who tries to make everything work even if I'm not sure whether I'm doing the right thing, by keeping him. I don't know how he feels right now because he doesn't reveal his true feelings that much nor that often. Maybe he's tired of me? Maybe I bore him? Or maybe he is interested in someone else? The guy whom he usually hangs out with? That's impossible! I suspect the other guy, though.

Clearly, I don't have a choice but to stick with this relationship as long as my patience can last. If he decides to dump me, I will have to accept it. Maybe he will. Maybe soon!

When that day finally comes, I will not resist my fate. At least, it's better than holding on to an unsure relationship alone. It would hurt, I know, but it's better than to get punished unendingly by his carelessness. I sometimes can't stand him; the way he treats me is somehow less like a girlfriend but more like a puppy that the owner isn't fond of and wants to get rid of but can't.

He: *"Sis, we're not boyfriend and girlfriend. Wake up, will you?"*

22

Team Single Forever Welcome

To love a good guy is better than trying to chase the best guy because he (*the best guy*) is too good to love. I had that experience when I was just a kid from the 10th grade. Oh my God, I can't believe I'm telling you my silly story. But here you go.

The 10th grade was a fun time because I enjoyed my life after I passed the 9th grade examination. My fate had changed dramatically the moment I saw a guy who was my senior.

He was perfect in so many ways, and many girls had a crush on him. I really hated those girls. I hate the fact that they were cute and adorable. They were like angels, but I was like a witch.

I couldn't compete with them.

Fortunately, my senior (*my crush*) was not interested in any of them. How did I know that? I might not be the most amazing girl at my school, but I knew every small detail about many amazing people, girls and guys alike. I was a professional stalker. You know?

I checked everything about him, so I knew he had no girlfriend at all. To me, he was like a prince living in his castle, and didn't know anything about the outside world. The saddest part was that he didn't know I also existed just next to his castle.

Sometimes I doubted whether he didn't know much about anything else besides study or he just didn't show it in public. That led me to further investigation.

My friends were not really helpful in anything else, but when it came to investigating stuff, they were very effective and useful. Together we hunted for any useful information about my crush.

At this point, I was sure he didn't know much about many things. I should say he was not interested in many things. The guy was a nerd, so to speak. The things that other kids loved were not on his list, and, in all fairness, what he liked could be a little strange to others too.

I started to feel something in my stomach.

"Oh, poor girl, he would never love you," I said to myself.

Simply, I was nobody, and the very chance to draw his attention was really slim. There was no way he could come to me. I mean, who would love a monkey like me?

It pains me to say this, but those girls didn't know how to quit. They always tried to talk to him. I was afraid that one of them would succeed and take him away from me.

I realized that I was jealous of the wrong people. I resented those girls even if I was sure he would never love them. I just didn't like them. Was I selfish?

Yes, I was selfish, but not too much, because I never looked after myself. I allowed my drama to dominate my thoughts. As a result, I needed to learn to hate my crush. I thought I would stop loving him if I could start to hate him.

See? I was a genius. I could come up with my own love formula, similar to math.

Love (+1) + Hate (-1) = Zero (0)

Did this formula work? Well, my math teacher just broke up with his girlfriend yesterday. We just had a small party last night. Do you get what I mean?

I'm not sure if the formula didn't work or I just sucked at everything. He didn't love me. That's the fact.

Did I hate him? Yes, I did.

Do I still hate him? No, I don't.

Do I still love him? Yes.

Is there any possibility that he would love me? None!

Now I know why you are reading **Impossible Crush**.

Welcome to *Team Single Forever*, sis!

23

Be a Good Person
Remember Him No More

People who have been tortured by loneliness have a way to show their own strength by being free and carefree. It's a matter of choice.

If you're one of them, let me express my heartfelt salutation. Be a good girl and never allow bad things to change your nature. You are naturally good, so be who you are. Believe in yourself. Believe that you are a good person. Believe that you deserve a good guy as well. If someone chooses to leave you, let him go. If he decides to go, then you let him follow his own choice.

You are good enough to love yourself, and you are not just an option for anybody. You have your own way, and you are valuable, so stop feeling bad about yourself.

Actually, I'm happy for you when you can face a nightmare, and you're still strong. You have the courage to face it. That I'm happy for you. You know who you are, and you love yourself. That I'm happy for you. You don't allow this experience to define who you are. That I'm happy for you.

If I face a similar situation, I might run away. You, on the other hand, don't run, and you choose to fight. You end this hardship by fighting against what's being thrown at you.

Be a good person and know your worth. Do not let anyone take away your self-worth. He might take some of the time from your life, but he can't take away your life. He only came to steal your valuable time because he was a thief. Let the thief go on his way, and remember him no more.

24

Then and Now

Then

After erasing my past memories, I would feel less stress and more freedom. Well, they were not necessarily bad memories, though. Some were good, and some were bad. Needless to say, if you didn't unlearn the bad ones (or even the good ones), how could you relearn better things? Learn to forget and forgive, and then you'd be free.

I would no longer think of you like I used to. I would probably remember you no more than just a person that faded away. I wouldn't wish to be with you again. All I wished was to be single and never to be disturbed by your drama again.

You chose to abandon me, so I let you go.

Now

After erasing my past, I feel less stress and more freedom.

I learn to forget and forgive, and now I'm free from pain.

I no longer think of anybody like I used to. I don't remember much about anyone. I don't care nor fear that anybody would hurt me, whatsoever. I simply don't care. I'm happy to be alone and free. That's a good life.

What else do I need?

25

A Good Student Improve

When you have a crush on someone, it is free of charge, so why don't you choose a better one? The one that helps you improve yourself. The one that can be the reason you change your bad habit. The one that can show you the beautiful sunshine.

I had a crush on someone who was so special like the moon, so beautiful, yet so far from me. Since I was just a little girl, it was impossible to reach him unless I was an astronaut.

Anyway, knowing that I loved him was enough for me. That's the starting point, and I decided to improve myself. I decided to become a good student in order to impress my crush because he's my classmate, and he's an outstanding student. I tried so hard I even outsmarted him. Now he hates me.

26

Careless or Care a Little Less? I Couldn't Care Less

I don't check Facebook Newsfeed, so I have no idea what my crushes are up to. Literally, I don't even care if they have a bad day or fail their exams. I don't want to know anything about them. I don't care if they get mad at me or not. Too busy to care. I like them, and that's all I need to know. For other things, I couldn't care less.

You might be wondering why, right? The truth is I have experienced enough not to care. I mean, caring too much only gives you a headache. Why do you have to care when your crush doesn't care about you?

Simply, you should do the same. Do you get what I mean? If you do, that means you don't care. If you don't, that also means you don't care. Or maybe you just don't understand what I'm talking about. Either way, I don't care.

Caring too much does hurt; caring too little doesn't, but not caring at all does no good either.

The question is: "Should you be careless or care a little less?"

27

A Good Boyfriend
The Story

This is the story about my girlfriend, who used to be my crush. My crush had a crush on someone, and she failed miserably. It is a sad story, and, as her current boyfriend, I am more than happy to tell you about it.

Once upon a time, there was a little girl named Anna. She had big beautiful eyes and a charming smile. Every guy loved Anna because of her smile. It's not because she always smiled like crazy. In fact, she's not that crazy. Her natural smile was the most beautiful thing. However, she rarely smiled. Those who were lucky could see how pretty she was when she was smiling.

Anna was a girl so loved by many and yet unwanted by those she loved. She had failed in her relationships so many times. She began to lose faith in any guy. She even believed that all guys were gays. Of course, that was not true. She told herself that she would not love anyone again until she found a guy. A nice guy who happened to be her senior.

She immediately fell in love with this stranger. Anna began her quest to find out more about this man. She wanted to know everything. She wanted to know who he was and where he came from. In short, she wanted to know him.

Long story short, after six grueling months, Anna decided to confess...

Now Anna is my official girlfriend.

He was her impossible crush, but I am her possible boyfriend. I accept her past as well as her flaws because nobody is perfect.

What is the moral of the story?

Moral: "*Never gossip about your girlfriend's crush. But if you do, make sure she would never find out.*"

28

A Good Sister
To My Sister

Don't wait to be perfect to love yourself. You can love yourself now.

Good things can happen to you, and you should be grateful. Nevertheless, the bad one could also happen. When it does, you should not react nervously. As long as you remain calmful and positive, nothing can put you in a harmful way.

I care about you, and I want you to remember that. But most importantly, I want you to remember that your mom loves you more than anything else in the world. She would be upset to know that you punish yourself because of someone's mistake. You should think about her. Think about how hard she has tried to raise you. Think about the devotion she has made just for you.

One day, you will finally meet the right person, and he is out there, waiting for you. Believe me, good things shall happen, and a good guy shall come. Be my good sister, and live a good life. Make your mom happy. Can you do that?

You'll understand the concept of happiness without relying on someone else's blessing. One day, you'll know that. You don't need permission from someone else to be happy.

In fact, happiness is your choice. If you choose to be happy, you will be happy. It's that simple. Don't you see? If you don't choose to be happy, then what else do you want to choose?

To be sleepy?

29

A Good Brother
Self-Realization

Self-love is important, but self-realization is the right thing to say at this point. Which point? A point where you see others more important than yourself, and you forget to see your own worth. You forget who you are, and you forget to be yourself because you're busy trying to please another person. When he rejects you, you feel bad, and you start to hate yourself. You look down on yourself when, in fact, you're the first person you should love.

You hate your own face because you think you're ugly, but you forget that your soul has always been a pure beauty that keeps you beautiful as a person.

You even reject your life when someone rejects your love. You begin to think that you're useless when your parents believe, very strongly, that you are the best thing they've ever had. You forget them. You forget how much they love you.

Now I want you to remember who you really are. Self-realization, my princess. It's important for you right now. Even Facebook can recognize your worth and good contribution to the world.

Why can't you realize your own worth in this world? You're not that useless, trust me. I also want to remind you that you are important, and it's impossible to reject this truth.

Love yourself, be yourself, and things shall happen again in a different way. What way?

Whatever, as long as it's not self-demoralizing.

51

30

Goodbye

Hi

When you hear the word "Hi," it is a good thing. When somebody doesn't have anything else to say besides "Goodbye," it is not a good sign. Goodbye usually means you won't get the chance to see or talk to that person, perhaps for a very long period of time. Goodbye is not good. You know? It's a sign of an impossibility!

This is why you should not say "Goodbye."

Then you ask, "What should I say?"

You can say whatever you want as long as it's not "Goodbye." Instead, you should say "Hi."

By the way, sometimes someone would text you and say: "Hi." Do you know why?

Wedding invitation. Again! [Damn it!]

I wonder if I would get an invitation when people get divorced.

PART 4
WHEN YOU TRY SO HARD

It's Going Nowhere!

31

Magic

You Are Unpredictable

I wish I could have a magic power to see through your heart, so I can attract you and capture your heart. I'm not trying to become a witch. Okay? When I know what you're thinking, it'll be easier for me to talk to you. At least, I'll know what to say instead of standing still, like a statue. Nobody likes a statue. Anyway, I'm trying to impress YOU!

Because you are unpredictable, I find it hard to talk to you. I'm afraid you'd get bored of me. As you can see, I'm not that good, nor am I confident enough to talk to anybody. Let alone to the person I like. I like him too much to risk my chance to bore him. Yeah, I'm talking about YOU!

You drive me crazy. Sometimes I smile alone, a lot, like never before, and that makes me happy. You give me a sense of purpose. That purpose is YOU!

32

Happiness
Looking at You

I wish I could tell you the truth that I fell in love with you. Since the first day we met, I guess. I can't describe how I feel, but all I know is that staying with you makes me feel safe even though you don't talk to me much. Usually, you leave me alone, and you talk with others.

Looking at you is my happiness. It does sound crazy, but it's true. You may not know it, but seeing you from the other side is a delightful moment. It's only a short moment, but it lasts forever in my heart. Okay, maybe not forever, but it could last longer than I can expect.

However, I am afraid that one day, if I tell you the truth, everything will end. I can't imagine the day you leave me just because I tell you that I like you.

I'd rather choose to have this secret happiness than pain. Even if it's just a little, I am still grateful. I just want to be happy, but I don't want to bother you.

Anyway, I also wish that one day you would know how much I love you, *stupid*.

33

Temporary
I Was Wrong!

I thought I was the only one who knew everything about you. All those things that you told me and all those stories that I knew. I thought that I knew all about you. Well, I was wrong. I was not the only one you told. In fact, you shared all your stories with everyone, especially girls. I hate those girls, but most importantly, I hate you. I was so disappointed. Did you know that?

Why do you have to be so transparent all the time? Can't you just keep some secrets to yourself? You make me feel special and give me temporary hope, only to make me hurt more. I hate you. I hate the fact that you are too carefree and careless. You are carefree, and you never care if your carelessness could hurt me or not. It does, very much so. I was wrong about you, and I'm still not sure how to read you. What am I supposed to do now? Give up on you? I won't!

34

Your Crush

Dummy

I don't know why you keep talking about your crush in front of me. You really hurt my feelings. Do you know that, dummy? I pretend that I like listening to you, but deep down, I feel miserable. You've never noticed my sorrow while you're telling me about her. You just don't care about me. Or maybe you're just dumb!

I know I like gossiping, but not about a crush of my crush, you idiot! You don't need to tell me how many times you miss her. You don't have to talk about her smell. Who in the world would want to know what kind of perfume she uses? Not me, obviously! I don't want to talk about her, and I don't want to know how beautiful or wonderful she is either. Honestly, I don't want to know anything about her, like ever! Okay?

Still, I have to pretend that I enjoy hearing from you. I wonder if you're just plain stupid, or you pretend that it's okay to tell me about your so-called perfect girl. Either way, I'm very disappointed with you.

Anyway, there is one exception about her that I want to know. I wonder how many times she farts per day.

Have you ever smelled that, smell catcher?

35

Stop It

Really, again?

I have a friend who is a good student. She's so good that I could rely on her. Don't get me wrong. I only rely on her while discussing the lessons. You can't count on her during the examination. She's a bad kid when it's time for the competition. Okay, she's not that bad. But she's an interesting woman. I almost fell for her sometimes. I'm only kidding. Not sometimes. All the time!

There was a time she came to me with exciting news. I thought she was going to tell me something really interesting. I thought wrong! Her so-called exciting news was a new book by her favorite author, whom she kept telling me over and over again.

I was like: "Really, again? Can you just stop it, sis?"

She never stopped. I didn't think she could stop. Like ever! That was when I started to dislike that guy (her favorite author). The more she talked about him, the less likely I would want to read his book. No joke, folks! I seriously hated to hear anything about him.

One day, I saw his name on Facebook, and then I Added Friend (to him). He Confirmed. A half month later, he replied to my story!

My Reply: loading...

36

The Same Question
Honey

Do you remember the question that you asked me? You asked me, "How to convince your crush to love you back?" Honestly speaking, I have no idea since I don't know how to convince you... (If you know what I mean!)

I try to ask him out all the time, but he often refuses. I don't know why, but I don't mind. I try to text him a lot. More than a lot, actually. He tries to ignore me too, I guess. Maybe he doesn't try. He just ignores! Despite many failing attempts, I wouldn't give up on this dimwit. Well, I'm not sure who's stupid. He? Or I? But sometimes he asks many stupid questions.

He asks: "How to convince your crush to love you back?"

It's funny when my crush asks me the same question I want to ask him. If I have the answer, I won't need to call him crush anymore. I would call him "Honey."

(Honey go where?)

37

Move On

Stay or Leave?

I decided to move on, and I tried to distance myself from you, many times, but it didn't work. Every time I tried to do so, you kept bringing me back. Why did you keep asking me to stay when I wanted to leave? Why did you keep pushing me away when I wanted to stay?

Maybe your heart wanted me to stay, but your head wanted me gone? Maybe you're unsure? Or what? You're a hard person to understand, and it's pretty scary. It's hard to be in this uncertain situation.

Do you want me to stay or leave? If you want me to stay, I will stay. If you want me to leave, I will leave.

Don't miss me when I'm gone.

38

Please Don't

It's Over

Don't look at me with those pitiful eyes. It's over. I gave my heart to you, but you never wanted it. You never noticed the pain that I had to carry. You never saw the tears rolling down my face. You never knew the fear that I had. The fear of losing someone I loved.

Don't tell me that you love me because it's over. If you really loved me, you would have done everything to keep me. You did nothing! You never cared about me.

Don't try to remind me about those memories. It's too late, baby. I know your trick. It worked before, but I won't fall twice. I'm not that stupid. Okay, I was stupid before, but not anymore.

Don't make another promise. It's too easy for you to break it, so you don't have to tell me. It used to sound convincing before, but not anymore. I used to believe you blindingly, but not anymore.

I won't believe your deception any longer, so please don't ever try that!

(And don't fart in front of me again!)

39

Your Dream
I'm Happy for You

I'm happy for you. Now you've found the girl of your dream. (Not a ghost in your dream, though.) But I'm happy even if I have to sacrifice a lot. My happiness. My time. My heart. My love. I want you to know that I will always stay by your side.

I hope she will love you like I do. I hope she won't hurt you, like you hurt me. I also hope she won't ignore you, like you ignore me. Unlike me, she's a lucky girl, and you're happy now. Please last long. Please do not take her for granted.

I know how it feels to be a toy for someone else. It ain't fun. It ain't pretty either. You should not give her the same experience I've got, but you should make her happy.

40

Busy

Sleep Well?

I know you are busy now. That's why you don't text me. It's been a week without your message, and I'm worried about you. I've been silent, but, actually, I want to know everything about you. Do you eat? Sleep well? Your day? Is it stressful?

I want to know everything, but all I can do right now is staring at my phone. Do you know that I'm waiting for your reply? Do you even know I ignore everyone else just to wait for your text? Maybe you don't know. And perhaps you won't even care if you do.

I hate to be the one who wastes your time, so I won't try to text you first. Believe me, it's hard, but I have no choice.

Why do you want me to try this hard and this much? Or am I just overthinking?

PART 5
WHEN YOU'RE DOWN

It's Disappointing!

41

High Expectation
Great Disappointment

When you expect so much from someone, usually you end up with great disappointment. If you don't believe me, you can ask people; everybody knows that. High expectation means great disappointment.

The man I loved was a good person, but our story wasn't good at all. The ending part was cruel, to me. Not to him, though. It began with a countdown trip. We went together, we came back together, and we got close. I thought we were in love already. What I didn't know was that he had fallen in love with my friend!

I fell in love with him, and I thought he knew that. He didn't. Nevertheless, we became close friends. So close that we could share many secrets. Except for one secret I never knew! I didn't know that he had a crush on my friend instead of me. Before I found out about this, I had expected him to confess to me. I was a fool, and I was very disappointed, because I expected a lot.

42

Jealousy

I Hate Those Girls

Well, I decided to stop checking your *Timeline* for many reasons. One of them is jealousy. You can say that I'm crazy. I get jealous when you get too close with those girls, but not me. Wait a minute. Who am I to you? A girlfriend? No.

Why do you have to be so nice?

I mean, you are friendly, and I know that, but you are too friendly. I'm sure those girls have a good feeling for you. If they don't, they wouldn't comment on many of your posts. I wish I could keep you away from them. I hate those girls.

They're not that pretty, but they know how to get your attention. That's what I hate. Unlike them, I'm not good at attracting you. It fills me with jealousy just to see their names. I can't wait to see how they react when we are in the relationship! (*Maybe in a million years.*)

43

Why Break Up?
Wait a Second!

You told me that I was your first crush, but you never told me that you had no feelings for me. You never told me that everything was wrong. Your action showed me that everything was okay. Suddenly, you left me. Why?

You told me that you wanted to be with me forever. But then you chose to abandon me. Why? Give me a good reason. Why can't we go through this together? Why can't you keep your promises? Why do we have to break up, crush?

Brain: *"Wait a second! How can you break up with your crush when you and he are not officially in a relationship?"*

44

Smile

Promise Me

You are so handsome when you are smiling at me, but you are the ugliest person on earth when you give that smile to someone else. I am not jealous...

Okay, I am jealous. I just hate it when you give that smile to many girls. Who are you? A superstar or what? Who are they? Your top fans or something? You don't have to smile at everybody. Nobody should ever see it. I alone should see your smile, and I alone could have your heart.

I know I sound desperate. Maybe a little crazy! Can't help that, though. Please promise me that you won't give this beautiful smile to anyone else again.

Promise me that. Okay?

Okay!

45

Dream

What about Me, Baby?

Do you believe in a dream? Do you believe that a dream can become a reality? I do believe that. I mean, I want to believe it since I usually dream about you.

In the dream, you say that you love me. Sometimes I wish to sleep early so that I can see you in my dream again. I'm not crazy. I just want to have as many dreams as possible and to see you as much as I can.

If my dream doesn't come true, you must take responsibility. You must confess to me, in reality. Do we have a deal?

Ghost: "What about me, baby?"

46

Let It Go

I Hate Myself

You believe you should be with her. You want her to be back. You still keep all her photos. You miss her every day. You still love your ex.

I hate that girl. I hate that I love you, and I hate to be the third person. I hate myself. I hate that feeling. I hate the fact that she came before me. I hate that you still love her.

You should, at least, give yourself another chance. A chance to love someone else. ME! You should forget her. The girl is gone, so you should not hold on to the ghost of your past. It's not worth it. You should let it go.

Let it go (Lo it get)!

47

Pain

I Can't Stop

Every day, I live in pain and suffering. Although I know that loving you is like torturing myself, I can't stop my feelings, still. I can't go back even if I know that loving the wrong person will make my life difficult. It's been this way since the beginning.

Sorry for dragging you into this dramatic situation, but I can't stop loving you. I can't force you, either. I suffer alone, and nobody knows what I feel and how I deal with this one-sided love. It's hard, and it sucks. I have no choice, and yet I don't blame you, either.

I choose to love you this much, and to live this way. You don't have to worry about me. Actually, I still doubt if you know how I feel about you because you don't seem to care much about me.

(*That's why I hate that bald girl.*)

48

Pretend
You Win

You never know how sad I am when you are with her. I pretend that I'm fine while, deep down, I'm completely broken. My heart is torn apart, by you, from the start. I act like I'm okay, but I'm not, and you know nothing about it. You never know, you never care, and you never ask. All you want to know is her. All you ask from me is her. What's so special about her, anyway? She's bald, and she's short, and...

Okay, I admit, she's cute. But you should never play with my feelings. Why do you have to trick me, just to get close to her? Why don't you tell me you love her?

I'm sad when you love my friend instead of me. You come to me just to get to her. Now you've got what you want. You win her heart, and I lose you to her.

I lost a battle before it even began. I lost you from the start. You were never meant to be mine. She was the one you wanted. She's your ideal person. She's special, and you love her, so you can go to her.

(*I wish both of you break up real soon!*)

49

Who Am I to You?
Okay!

Sometimes you act like we are more than friends, but sometimes you act like you don't care. It seems like I think and care too much. You really drive me crazy, and your actions make me more confused. Moreover, your words, sometimes harsh and sometimes sweet. I have a hard time trying to understand you. Now I guess I really need to know something.

Who am I to you? A sister? A friend? A stranger? Or else? Is there any possibility for us? A chance to be in the relationship?

Yes?

No?

Okay? Okay!

50

Wrong

Right

Do you think action speaks louder than words? Wrong! I am good at acting. I can act like I am happy or crazy, but, in my mind, I am really sad. I am unhappy because of you.

Do you think having a crush is a fun thing? Wrong! I have a crush on you, and it's not fun. Each night, I can't sleep well because I keep thinking about you. I have to stop myself from checking your *Timeline*. It really hurts my *meow* feelings whenever you post something unrelated to me, or, even worse, when you talk about someone else.

Do you think I hate you? Wrong! I love you.

Do you think I want to slap you? Right! I sure do!

PART 6
TRY NOT TO CRY

It's the Turning Point!

51

No Longer
Expect

You are a history, remembered no longer. You are nobody, and everything you do is appreciated no more. Never ever expect anything else. Expect not what you want because you will never get it. You will never find peace with yourself because of your selfishness.

You are just the history, and she doesn't care about this unwanted history anymore. She tries to forget everything about you. Not to mention how you made her feel. She got lost because of you, so you lost her. That's fair.

You expect her to love you the same way she did? How can you expect someone, who had invested so much love in you but lost so much time with you, to believe you again?

She has no more faith in you because you always make her feel unsure of what to do, and you make her feel unsafe in this unstable and uncertain relationship. How can you expect her to stay? How can you expect her to love you? This is insane.

This is impossible, and you are unbelievable because you screw up everything. I can't believe you still keep asking her to stay. Why don't you let her go? She has had it enough. She is so fed up with your pathetic love. Let her go. Let her find the right guy who can protect her heart.

52

Heart Killer

Stay Away

*You had sworn to protect her heart only to destroy her happiness later on. You are a heart killer, and you know that. If you want to protect her heart, you just need to do one thing: **"Stay away from her."***

The longer she's with you, the more dangerous it becomes. The more she loves you, the more she gets hurt. The more she cares, the more she suffers. You are the reason she is depressed. What else do you want?

Do you want to see another girl suffering because of you? Do you want another victim? You should stay away from her, and that's the best option you've got.

Stay away, and don't ever come back!

53
Programmed
Not to Love

You are programmed not to love and not to get hurt by love. You have no heart. You have no hatred. You have no feelings for love. You only know one thing about it. Never fall in love again. To love is to get hurt, and to be loved is to hurt, and you know these consequences. That's why you need to program your mind not to love again.

People think only the robot is programmed not to love or hate. They think that the robot is different from human beings because it has no heart. They forget that many people feel the same way. Some people prefer to be like a robot because they want to get rid of love and hatred.

You should know that you might bring destruction to her world when you decide to accept her. You can never love anyone again, or you will destroy yourself. Perhaps, you would destroy someone else's life as well.

Now you listen and you listen well. You can never love anyone again. You hear me?

It's better to let her suffer now than later. You know what could happen next if you choose to accept her. She will suffer much more than this.

When she has a crush on you, she knows that she is taking a risk. A risk might hurt her, or it might not, but the moment you accept her, she will definitely face a bigger problem. One day, you will leave her, and that will be the day you break her heart just like you have done to other women. When that day comes, you'd better pray she wouldn't think too much, because sometimes overthinking could kill a person.

54

Selfish

You Distance Yourself

"You ignore her, and you talk with others. You treat her like the third wheel. Like a toy. You choose her only when you have no other options available. You even pretend that she never exists while, in fact, she's right there in front of you. You distance yourself from her when she really needs you. You only think about yourself because you're selfish. Keep being selfish, and you'll live alone for the rest of your life."

To Every Woman Reading This

You should become independent. Why? Because asking another person to give you happiness is a sure way to depression.

You should be happy. Why? Because overthinking is a sure way to unstable mood and restlessness.

You should be true to yourself. Why? Because to become an option for someone else is not delightful. To change yourself in order to please him is to compromise your value. You either lose your self-worth, or you lose a person who cares little about you. You choose!

You should be strong. Why? Because to be weak is not who you are. (*I'm being biased here, but just be strong. Okay?*)

Life is a long road, but to walk alone is better than to walk with the wrong person.

Crush: *"But, sometimes to walk with the wrong person (me) is better than to walk alone, if you're walking near a pagoda. If you know what I mean."*

55

Hurtful

You Are with Someone Else

"Now you are with someone else, and I am alone waiting for the forgotten promise. I have no right to request anything because what's done is done. I just hate it whenever I think about you; it's freaking hurtful. I don't ever want to think about everything that we had together, but I can't stop thinking about it."

From a Woman Who Got Hurt

The message that I want to send to other women is very simple. When you meet a man, who is so stubborn and self-centered, you simply have two options. To stick with your own decision (to be with him) or to lose him!

If you choose to stick with him, you should give him enough time and space. Let me explain it to you. Giving people what they want is not always easy, especially when it means you have to sacrifice a part of your value. I myself have experienced this. The man whom I love is stubborn. He's so stubborn nobody can change him. Unfortunately, I fell in love with this guy, so I accept that part of his flaw. To me, it's a flaw, but to him, it's his identity. He's not going to lose it, I'm sure. I don't want to force him to change that either. To ask him to be a little more like me is like to ask a cat to be a little more like a dog. I accept that we both are different in some ways, so I'm willing to give him enough time to see how we can deal with our differences. Eventually, he has noticed my value (as a woman), so he tries to understand more about me too. We're making progress.

You have to know that a relationship is not always pretty. It's more like a person. When you wake up in the morning, without makeup, you would look like Sun Ou Kong. At least, that's how you feel, right? When you go out, and with perfect makeup, you would look like Thang Cheng. Wait, what? Okay, that doesn't make any sense.

What I'm trying to say is that you should accept the fact that your relationship is not always perfect or pretty. There are times when you cry. There are times when you laugh. There are times when you laugh and cry. Well, I'm not sure if you can laugh and cry at the same time. The point is you should try to understand your partner. Sooner or later, he'll understand more about you too. Been there, done that. Believe me, you won't feel guilty for getting mad at him for no reason. If you don't understand how he lives his life, yeah, you'll get mad even when he's in the toilet. A friend of mine cried hard almost every night because her boyfriend pooped long and often, in the toilet, and he left her call all the time.

I was like: "*Sis, he needs to poop. Stop getting mad at your boyfriend for pooping.*"

Well, just for the record, she did listen to my advice. They got married, eventually. Now both of them are divorced already, after a month of sweet marriage. Maybe the guy farts too much too. I guess!

My boyfriend has a different problem. He doesn't fart that much nor that often. At least, not that I know of. Anyway, he's a super-duper stubborn kid. He doesn't like to take advice from anyone. He doesn't want to listen to nobody. Despite that, I get stuck with this relationship because I choose to stick with my own decision (to be with him).

If you choose the second option, which is to lose someone you love, then it'll be easier than what I have mentioned above. All you need to do is block him. End of the story!

56

Problem
The Same

While everybody is having a good time, I have to deal with my own depression caused by the same problem. I have to face this situation again and again, because of the same person. YOU!

I just want to run away from everyone because I feel like a loser, but I can't. In fact, I've always felt that way ever since you left. I hate myself for remembering what you've forgotten. I hate you because you put me in this dark place. It's scary and painful. I hate to be the victim, but I can't shake off my pain and anger. I wish I could think of a better way to live my life, but I can't find one. The only way to deal with my life right now is to avoid talking about it. Except for now! I can't stop thinking about you, nor can I avoid talking about us. It's too much to bear. The heavy burden of loyalty is a cruel penalty a silly person (like me) has to pay.

57

What Should I Do?
Hope

I still remember our good things together. We were the happiest couple, and every day was sweet, like lemon. Okay, that's not sweet. But we did have a good time together. We had many good memories. I don't want to erase them, because they give me hope. Because of this hope, I keep waiting for your answer. The answer that never comes! I'm not sure how long. It's impossible to know!

The longer I wait, the longer it seems. There is no sign of possibility. The possibility of reuniting two souls. It's impossible to happen!

I don't understand why I'm still giving myself hope. The hope that you'll be back. It's impossible to hope for that!

What should I do? Should I keep waiting (*or should I burn your house*)? Maybe it's possible?

58

Daydreaming
A Chance

Sometimes you make me feel that I could have a chance to be with you. When I really try, I realize that I have been daydreaming. You have so many good women who love and care about you, and they are much better than me. Unlike them, I am nothing in your eyes.

I should not aim too high because I never deserve such a great person like you. You are very high, and I am so low you could never see. I am far from good while you are too good to love me. By destiny, we are not possible!

You will have a great life without a silly girl like me. I wish you all the best and find the love of your life.

(But don't fall in love with my friend. Okay?)

59

Now

Again

My friend changes girlfriends almost every time I meet him. I am amazed because he could move on so fast. I meet him once a month, and, believe me, I frequently see different faces. I'm like: "*Wow, again?*"

Is he that good at flirting or I just get stuck in my past? I mean, I really admire him because love doesn't hurt a man like him. He just doesn't care. He is really strong, I could say.

While I was very depressed because of my breakup, my friend was chatting with a new crush and establishing a good relationship already. I was sort of jealous. If you know what I mean.

I wish I could move on fast like my friend does. I wish I didn't need to blame myself every day. I wish I could stop my fear. I wish I could be carefree.

I wish for everything, and yet I never want to do anything about it because I focus on the past too much for too long. The misery. The failure. And everything!

Actually, everything is not that bad, but I make it sound really bad. I guess I should change my thought, right?

What's done is done, and there's nothing I can do about it. I should let it go. I should expect no more from it. I should focus on something else. Something that is truly important. I have neglected my own happiness because I still believe that my happiness can exist only when that person is with me.

But wait, which one?

It doesn't matter who she is. What really matters is that I repeat the same mistake with different people. I guess the real problem is myself.

Now I know. I know that it is time to move on, and it is the right time to consider the real relationship and stop getting hurt by the one I love.

I have messed up my life really badly, and that's why I'm afraid of a new relationship. I believe that many people have experienced the same frustration. They could be out there waiting for the right answer to fix their puzzled lives.

You should stop waiting for the answer from others. Stop waiting for the miracle to happen to you because you are your own miracle. Your life will be better if you stop trying to keep your own past. It will be brighter if you start to live your present life.

Nobody can hurt you more than yourself. But guess what, nobody should love you more than yourself. You need to love yourself more than this. You don't have to wait to be perfect. You need to love yourself from now on. I really mean NOW!

60

Loud and Clear
Seriously?

Why did you do that to me? You really made me feel so embarrassed the way you did what you did. I was there to witness those moments. I couldn't believe what I saw. In fact, I didn't see it. I just... Oh God, I don't want to talk about it. It's so crazy and ridiculously funny. It was funny to others, and maybe to you too, I wasn't sure. But I was very sure, in the name of crush, it was impossible to see what I saw. You made yourself look like a fool, and you also dragged me into this mockery. My friends always laughed at me, and I couldn't talk to them about you because of what you had done. Nuts!

By the way, the endeavor to seek attention from you was my ultimate goal, and yet I had undergone a life-changing experience the moment you did what you did, although it was not intentionally towards me. But it was a clear message; it showed that we were impossible to love each other. You sent this message, loud and clear, to me and people around you... (*I don't know what to say.*)

Did you think I was just a tree or what? Or was I invisible to you? Was I just the air? You didn't mean to hurt me, but your action did. Whenever I think about it, it only causes me to stop thinking about you.

Maybe you thought I was nothing to you? Or were you not aware that I was there when you did what you did? It hurt more than breakup or cheating, you know? It's really too much, and I couldn't stand that.

I couldn't stand there and listen to all this...

I don't know what to say. Maybe you thought you were the only person living in this world? You forgot to notice others around you, and you never saw me, I knew that for sure.

Why did you do that? I mean, really, twice?

You farted, so loudly and so clearly.

You farted twice, and I was there to witness those crazy moments. In the class. And while I was standing behind you. Seriously?

PART 7
TRY NOT TO MEOW

It's Just a Joke

61

See First

Dear Crush,

Actually, I'm an anti-social media person, but I post a lot of stuff because I want to make sure you are fine. I mean, I don't want you to be depressed. Why?

When someone gets depressed, she might deactivate her own account and isolate herself from others. See? That's why I must post something to make sure she's still alive. Get it?

Only *See-First* crush could understand this logic.

Crush: *"In fact, you're the reason I'm depressed."*

(**Suggestion from Tony the Cat**: *Turn off the notifications from social media apps, for one week. If it doesn't meow you, then nothing else can meow you.*)

62

Son?

Dear Crush,

When we first met, I called you *sister*, and you called me *brother*. It was normal to call each other that way. Later on, you called me *sis*, and I called you *bro*. I didn't mind being a sister as long as you liked it.

Time flew, and our relationship changed. You liked me, and I liked you. You told me, and I told you. Now I call you *baby* and you call me *son*.

Wait a minute!

Baby and son? What does it mean?

(**Warning from Tony the Cat**: *Believe me, I tried this with Isabellu. I called her bro-meow, and she slapped the meow out of me. It didn't work, folks!*)

63

Tall

Dear Crush,

Why are you so tall? Have you ever bothered to look down when you are walking? Have you ever realized that somebody is looking up to you? I mean, literally looking up. She is just a little girl with small eyes, but she has a big heart. Believe me, she's cute also. You know what they say, *"A short girl is cute."*

To be honest, you are a cool guy, except for when you are uncool. You are naturally a good person, but sometimes you act like a fool. You are smart, but you're dumb at the same time. You can't figure out that this silly girl has a crush on you. *What an idiot!*

But why are you so tall? I mean, what do you eat? You eat rock or something?

(**Tip from Tony the Cat**: *To become smart, you just need to eat cat food. Trust me, you'll be as sharp as a meow.*)

64

Now I'm Cute

Dear Crush,

Because of you, I have to eat in the morning. You used to tell me that breakfast was very important. I believed you, so I forced myself to get up early to find something to eat. Now having breakfast in the morning has become my habit. My mom is very happy when I eat more. I used to eat like a cat, though.

Because of you, I have to eat a meal in the middle of a busy day. As you know, I'm the busiest human being on Earth, but I have to eat because you told me that I should eat more.

Because of you, I have to eat dinner. Before knowing you, I didn't eat rice in the evening. I ate something else (usually a snack) with my friends, and my stomach got full till midnight. My habit has changed, thanks to you.

Because of you, I become chubby. I don't want to use the word "*fat*" because it sounds too ugly. Well, I'm a little ugly, but not too ugly, right? Right?

Therefore, to say that I'm chubby is better because it sounds pretty cute. Okay, now I'm cute. Whatever!

But you have to be responsible. Nobody will love me when I'm fat like this, so you have to love me.

You MUST!

(**Note from Tony the Cat:** *Believe me, you're not ugly. You're unique. You get what I meow?*)

65

Noodles?

Dear Crush,

Since we first met, I've been crazy about you. I think of you all the time. Do you know that? Your smile. Your voice. Your action. Everything you say or do just makes my heart beat faster. I miss you all the time.

I couldn't sleep well at night because of you. Do you know that? I often check your *Timeline*, and I want to know everything about you.

I couldn't eat anything because of you. Do you know that? I couldn't eat rice. Only noodles!

Crush: "*Why only noodles?*"

(**Question from Tony the Cat**: *Meow. Why not fish?*)

66

Do You Miss Me?

Dear Crush,

Do you miss me? If you don't miss me, I will stop talking to you. But wait, since when did you talk to me? I mean, you don't even know who I am. Yes, I know, I know. I know who I am. But do you know that I have a crush on you? You don't. I know that.

I thought you were smarter than this. I thought you could smell it when a person has a crush on you. Clearly, you're not that good at smelling.

Crush: *"Am I a dog to you?"*

(Reaction from Tony the Cat: *I can't smell it, either. Your meowing style is lame.*)

67

I Wish

Dear Crush,

If your wish could become a reality, what would that be? If you could meet the girl of your dreams, what would you say to her?

For me, I wish to see her every day because her face is so beautiful. She is so charming that everyone wants to become her possible crush. Literally, she's an angel.

If I had a chance to tell her, I would say: **I love you.**

She*: "Thanks to editing apps for turning an ugly monster into a pretty angel. And I love myself too."*

(**Idea from Tony the Cat**: *Bro, don't tell your crush that you meow her. Show her! Do you meow what I mean?*)

68

I'm Tired

Dear Crush,

I wish I could *uncrush* you. Why? Because I'm tired of stalking you every day. I'm tired of trying. Trying and trying, without any result.

I wish you would notice me. Yeah, I know. I know. A notification about someone is like a drop of rain in the ocean. You are flooded by many things from many people, and it's easy to forget just another unimportant person. I'm not important to you, I know that, but at least, you should notice my effort.

In short, you're a cruel person. I wish you could...

(*Oh, and I wish your crush would uncrush you too so that we will be...*)

Do you know what I want to say?

(**Advice from Tony the Cat**: *Meow. Meow. Meow.*)

69

Another

Dear Crush,

Why do you have to ignore me? Do you know that I am disappointed? I love you, and you're the only one in my dream, but you don't care. You never care about me. You never want to see my face.

Am I a ghost or something? Why do you have to run away from me? Are you afraid of me or what?

Now I decide to delete you from my heart, and I'll find another impossible crush. Then I'll be heart-broken again!

Crush: *"No. I'm not afraid of you. I'm afraid of your mom."*

(**Comment from Tony the Cat**: *Even a blind cat can tell. You're a terrible meow.*)

70

How Soon?

Dear Crush,

Don't regret it when I no longer chat to you...

Wait a second, have you ever *Seen* my chat? As far as I know, you never have. Maybe in my dream, you have.

Maybe in my dream, you try to flirt with me. Or just the opposite, maybe. I don't know.

Don't regret it when I stop flirting with you. Don't try to stop me from leaving you. Okay?

Crush: "*How soon will you leave?*"

(**Regret from Tony the Cat**: I regret that *I didn't flirt with that cat Kamelu when I had the chance.*)

PART 8
TRY NOT TO FLIRT

It's Your Choice!

71

An Idiot

Like a Song

I am up on the roof, thinking of you, day and night. Day and night, baby. I know I'm blind and crazy. I know I'm silly and addicted too, but I don't know if you know that I like you. I really do!

I'm so in love with you, and God knows I do. Only you could make my dream come true. Only you! (*And a friend of yours too!*)

Does it sound like a song? I'm like a singer now. Can you believe that?

Love can turn a man into a cow. I meant to say that love can push me to sing like a cow.

Only an idiot would flirt this way!

Well, maybe I'm an idiot?

72

No More
Only the Truth

"I need only the truth, not the lie that you try to tell. Tell me no more about the promises which you intend to break. Tell me no more about the stories which are fake. Fake the stories no more, and no more fake love. If you can't love me anymore, just leave. Don't worry about me. I'll be fine."

Never

I dreamed of being with you once again, but it's only a dream remaining untrue in reality. I never lost my faith in you. I never lost faith in us. But you did. You lost faith in me. You lost faith in our relationship. I accepted our fate (breakup) and moved on.

From the time we were together, never once had I stopped loving you. Never once had I thought we would become strangers. Never in my mind would I believe things could end up this way. You had chosen your path and walked a separate way from mine, so I let you go.

I let you go because I love you. I still do, with all my heart.

When we were together, we were more than happy, and, for once, my life had seen the light of joy. I had never thought about anything else other than to spend the rest of my life with you. Suddenly, your love faded away, and you walked away from this relationship.

I accept it, and live accordingly. To live as a decent person and to be a loyal partner!

73

Brand
Coffee

The coffee is similar to your crush. Sometimes you need it, but sometimes you don't. Sometimes you drink it, but sometimes you don't. Sometimes you crave for it, but sometimes you don't. Your crush is like coffee, so much addictive and bitter-sweet. Your crush could make your heart beat fast also. Just like the coffee!

Some people prefer brand, brand crush while some don't really care about beauty. Okay, it sounds like a cliché. People do care about beauty, but different people have different types of crushes. Some people love a short girl; some love a chubby girl. Some prefer a sweet lady while some only see the gentle one in their eyes. Some people are attracted to a heartbreaker.

If your heart is not ready, try not to flirt!

74

In the Middle of the Rain?
Are You Serious?

Do you really think your love story is like a movie? You are dreaming. It ain't like a movie. What do you want? You want to tell your crush about your feelings in the middle of the rain? Are you serious?

Let me give you a piece of advice. When you and your crush are under the rain together, all you need is an umbrella. What else do you expect?

Holding her hand? Believe me, she only wants to get home as soon as possible. She knows that it is more dangerous when you hold her hand under the rain.

Because the thunder doesn't care about your love confession. Okay?

Thunder: *"That's right, honey. Go home, or ⚡ ⚡ ⚡ ⚡"*

75

Hi

Doing?

Hi, Crush.
Doing?
No chat with SS (*Someone Special*)?
5 Minutes Later...
Facebook User (You can't reply to this conversation)

76

We Don't Talk
Like a Cow

We don't talk anymore. No, we don't talk anymore.

We don't talk like animals. No. No. We don't talk like animals, no more, no more. Okay, now I sound a lot more like an animal. But that doesn't matter because we don't talk anymore.

We don't know each other anymore. You don't know me, and I don't know you, so we are strangers. But we don't talk anymore. We don't text anymore. And we don't date anymore.

We don't talk like cows anymore.

But we do sing like a cow.

"*Mor. Mor. Mor. Mor.*"

77

I Miss Him

Who?

Me: I miss him.
My Friend: Which one?
Me: The one you told me yesterday.
My Friend: Who?
Me: Your crush!

78

End of the Story
I Don't Believe That Either

I stopped loving my crush already. I swear to my new unborn crush. I no longer like him, but I still check his *Timeline* almost every day. Do you know why?

You would say, *"Only a ghost would believe you. How can you stop loving someone but still want to know about him?"*

I keep stalking him every day because I want to know more about his sister. The truth is I have a crush on the sister of my crush. End of the story!

Ghost: *"I don't believe that either."*

79

Uncool

It's Okay

It's okay if you're short, but don't be too short. Okay? When we talk, it's difficult for me to look at you. I mean, I have to look down.

It's okay if you're uncool, but don't be too ugly. Okay? When we go anywhere together, people wouldn't believe that we are a couple. Because I'm ugly already. Like the saying, "*An ugly guy belongs to a cute girl.*"

Be my cutie forever and ever. Get it, *Shorty Cutie*?

It's okay if you're shy, but don't be too shy. When we meet our friends, they will talk ill about us. So instead of letting them gossip about us, we should gossip about them. Understood?

Now you've understood, so we will meet each other in a million years!

80

I Will

Nobody

When you have nobody, I want you to remember me. I will be there for you when you need somebody. When nobody loves you, I will. When nobody cares about you, I will. When nobody believes in you, I will.

I will stay by your side, as always. I will make you happy, as much as I can. I will never ever let you down. I will be your reminder. I will be your motivator. I will be whatever you want me to be. I want to be somebody. Somebody that you need.

(**Note**: *Nobody is not a ghost, because sometimes a ghost does have a body.*)

PART 9
TRY NOT TO CONFESS

It's Not Helpful!

81

Unplanned
Unexpected Affection

I met this man who was a nice guy. We chatted quite a lot, and I could tell that he meant well. He didn't flirt like most guys I had met before.

Unexpectedly, I had a good feeling for this guy. I liked him. This unplanned affection would lead to the unpredictable flirtation, if not the confession, by me.

I liked him, I knew. I liked texting with him because he was not only a good person, but he also had a sense of humor. He could make you laugh even when he's not trying to be funny. Well, I don't want to use the word "weird" to describe the guy, but he's a funny man with a funny personality, and it's fun to talk with him. He allowed me to ask him all kinds of questions. He also knew I did sound ridiculous sometimes, but he still managed to keep our conversation smooth. By the way, he did laugh when I made some jokes, but I wasn't sure if he was laughing at the jokes or at me. Whatever that might be, I couldn't care less. All I cared about was an honest conversation, and he also knew that, enough to respect that about me.

As a matter of fact, we were having a good time, mostly with little filter in our conversation, but he fully respected me and avoided asking anything too personal or too embarrassing. When it came to embarrassing himself, he wasn't shy to talk about his childhood or things of that nature. There was a time when he talked about a fond memory of his childhood, and he asked me about mine. I told him a story of my childhood too.

I found it to be refreshing to hear about many things without a filter. He didn't try to sound like a perfect boy in his childhood. In fact, he tried to humble himself. I respected that about him, to be honest.

You can tell when someone is being honest or not by listening to how he tells you about his childhood stories. I was convinced that he was an honest guy. Meanwhile, I was sort of unsure why I changed my mind that fast about a person and a relationship. Before I met him, I used to dislike it when someone (guy) tried to approach me, mostly by chat. I kept my life as private as possible and avoided strangers. I even blocked some along the way.

Previously, I thought the same way about him; I wanted to avoid talking with this guy. It's surprising how my mind had changed that fast. I thought that it was too soon to say that I loved the guy, but I knew that there was a small voice in my head that kept telling me many good things about him. Maybe that small voice was a little biased, but I sort of wanted to agree with it.

Maybe I loved him? No, that can't be possible. Well, I wasn't sure.

Either he was an expert in heart stealing, or he was the one. Either way, my life was going to change. For better or for worse, I did not know yet. The thing I knew couldn't explain how I felt about him because it was too quick and unexpected.

Maybe I should slow down my feelings. I should talk with him less, or I would end up telling him the truth and risking embarrassing myself. I don't want him to find out about this. I

will take it slowly and wait to see if he's really the one. I must not reveal my true feelings too soon. I...
(*Messenger Notification*)

82

Beautiful
Addicted

I have lost my good moments when I don't talk with you. I feel like I'm addicted to the way I feel about you. And I can't stop smiling whenever I think of you. Do you know how wonderful it feels when I think about the times we chatted? It is beautiful, and I must admit that you are the most wonderful person I've ever met. I really mean it.

It is more than a sad feeling when I learn that I couldn't talk with you anymore, but I hope that you are doing fine and having a good time.

I confess that I love you, but I should also confess that you stop talking to me because of my confession. I'm an idiot!

83

The Same Trap
I Know

I know you are frustrated. I know you are unsure. I know you are doubtful. But please let me reassure you. Nothing can hurt you more than your own thinking. Nobody could break your heart if you don't allow him to. You have the choice to make. You either choose to let him fool you, or you choose to see things through and maintain your own determination. When you are determined to stay the same, nobody can change you. On the other hand, if your belief is shaken, then it's easy to become negative and depressed.

You should always remain undisturbed despite any temporary excitement. It could be tempting too, but you don't have to fall into the same trap. What trap? It is the trap of a temporary relationship.

This kind of relationship could be exciting at first, but it doesn't last that long. In the end, one shall leave and one shall suffer. More often than not, you are the one who would suffer.

Suggestion from *Tony the Cat*: **Try not to accept too soon; it's the same trap.**

84

To Confess or to Continue?
A Virgo

The guy I like is Virgo. In my opinion, a Virgo is the type of person who doesn't care about anyone. Simply, he's too busy to care about me. I feel that he's lost interest in me, too fast. He texts me, still, but it's always late-night text. And I mean really late. I don't mind that, honestly, but I don't like it when he keeps it so long before he decides to text me. I mean, sometimes he gets home early, but it takes him, at least, an hour to text me. Instead, the guy posts something on Facebook, and I'm like: ... *He acts like it's a normal day.*

We still talk daily, but the gap makes me feel less important. Maybe I expect too much and too soon, although I never say anything to him. He is stupid sometimes. He doesn't know that I constantly wait for his text. Or maybe he does? The truth is I don't know what to do. To tell him the truth or to hide my true feelings? To confess or to continue to be in this mess?

85

I Won't Tell
Being Alone

Maybe I have been alone for too long and no longer want to change this lifestyle. I get used to being alone, thinking alone, eating alone and going everywhere alone. It's really hard for me to believe that I actually deserve to be loved by anyone. The scars from my past are too big and too obvious to hide. Nobody could accept a person like me. I know that.

I believe that, so I couldn't risk losing you because you are far more important than those people who left me. Yet I don't want you to leave me one day, so I must keep it secret that way and never reveal this to you or others.

I did give you some clues, though. If you are smart enough, then you would know because there's nothing really complicated to understand.

True feelings! Sometimes I get bored of talking with you, but I just keep listening because I don't want to hurt your feelings. Plus, I love listening to you more. This is why I choose to listen more than comment.

Anyway, I really enjoy most of the conversations that we have. I like it when you tell me about your life at home, your friends at school, and everything else. You tell me about how you deal with loneliness when your friend doesn't pay attention to you more than her boyfriend. You tell me all about it, and I can learn more about you, at least, in a way that I can relate to.

Still, there is no way I will tell you the truth. I love you, but I won't tell you that. You will need to find out by yourself, *Potato*.

86

Dream

My First Time

It's my first time seeing you in my dream, but it feels like a reality. I almost believed that it was real. I thought you knew that I...

You told me about your mom, and I thought you were having a hard time with your life at school and at home. You told me that your mom had opposed every move you made and everything you did.

Honestly speaking, I couldn't remember when I started to like you. That feeling, you know, when you really like someone very much despite the fact that you could only see her through social media. Yeah, you really make me insane sometimes. Anyway, do you know who you are?

I can't answer that question, for I'm not really sure if you're reading it right now. All I know about you is...

(Forget it. I'm not going to tell!)

I've decided not to tell you about what I'm really thinking. Well, not directly or officially. It's better if you remain my impossible crush because I won't be able to hurt you, just so you know.

I just want you to be happy, and that's all I want. Previously, I had wanted so many things and expected so much that it turned out to be very disappointing. At this point, I don't have the courage to try that again because... (*I don't know what to say*). All I can say is that **I love you**. I want you to be happy because you deserve a good life. **A life without me.**

87

Courage
Oh My God

The happiest moment is when she reacts *laugh* on my post.

I was like: "*Oh my God!*"

Is it okay to love you? I'm really happy every time I think of you, but I'm not brave enough to tell you what I've always wanted to tell. The fear of losing you always gets in my way, and I get stuck with it.

I need the courage to tell you about it, but I may need more time to prepare myself. I may need to wait a little longer. I need you to promise that you won't be too shocked.

You have to promise me that. Okay?

88

Your Name
Do You Know That?

I have to admit that we have shared a strong connection and affection. I have always enjoyed your company, and your presence has always been the greatest medicine that can heal my wounded heart.

I begin to get addicted to seeing your name at the top of my chat list. When I check my *messenger*, you are the first person I want to see. If I don't see your name, I will throw my phone away. Okay, I don't throw my phone away.

We both understand how it feels to be useless. Be that as it may, when I talk with you, that feeling simply disappears, and I believe you have brought me a new purpose to live in this life. Now it is my turn to show you the new way to stop devaluing yourself.

You are amazing. Do you know that?

Who are you?

89

Hope
I Won't Confess

I don't want to give much hope to myself because I usually fail when I expect too much.

I know you only think of me as a friend. I know you don't want to be more than this. I know you have your own type. The fact of the matter is I'm not your type, and I can never be the one in your eyes.

I won't confess to you.

(*Well, maybe I should confess to your friend instead?*)

90

Your Voice
When I Wake Up

When I wake up, the first thing I remember is my phone. The first person I think of is you. I want to know what you texted me the night before that. I want to know and read every word you send even though many things you say are the same. Like the old day before that.

Your words are very sweet, and yet I'm not tired of hearing what you say. I love the way you tell me about everything. You are just so sweet. You know that?

And your voice. Oh God, I'm so in love with your voice. It's just adorable and charming. Like the sound of a cow!

PART 10
DO NOT TRY

Some Tips!

91

To Disturb

I Shouldn't

Even if we don't talk like we used to, I still want to know everything about you. I want to know if you still feel stressed each day after work. Still dislike your workplace environment? Still want to quit that job?

I know you have had so much stress from everything around you, and I hate to become another problem for you. You have a lot going on in your life, and yet I still put more pressure on you. I'm sorry. I really mean it. I hope your life will be better. I hope you can find the solutions for the problems at your workplace. I have faith in you because you are a strong person. Nothing can stop you; I know that. Try your best. You will be able to go through this.

Don't worry about it. You will find the solutions.

Be positive and believe in yourself. I believe in you. I believe that you will achieve your big dream in the future. You are the future of your family. Make your parents proud. Make the rest of your life the best of your life. Be free and be an independent person. Be great. You are great. You will find something that you are looking for. Just keep searching.

It's okay to be alone for a while. At the right time, you will appreciate the time with others once again. Now you should follow your mind.

Meanwhile, I shouldn't disturb you. As a matter of fact, I should be gone already.

92

To Wait

I Should Stop

I remember the time when I was waiting for your text, asking me if I had gotten home yet. Now it's different because you are getting busier and busier. You won't have time to text me like you used to. I can understand that, and I won't blame you. From now on, I should stop waiting for your text.

I should, instead, focus on my life and try to think less of you. I hope I can do that even though it's hard, I know. It's hard when I try to focus on something else, instead of you. Whenever I try to forget about you, I feel stressed and unable to rest. It's annoying. You know?

Nevertheless, I shall not wait for you. I shall never expect too much like I used to. Time will take away my stress and restlessness, and I shall be fine.

93

To Cross the Line
Who Is She?

We have a good time together, but we have a boundary. I have to admit that sometimes I want to cross the line. Sometimes I wonder if she likes me or not. Does she feel the same way about me as I feel about her? I really want to ask her about it, but I am afraid she will stop being good to me if she finds out that I actually like her so much.

Being her friend is my most delightful feeling, for I can talk to her. Anyway, sometimes I tend to talk too much, and I'm not sure if she gets bored or she is glad to listen to my stories. She even laughs when I tell her my funny stories. She makes me very curious, and I really want to know what's going on inside her mind.

Does she know that I love her? Maybe she pretends that she doesn't know? Does she like me too? Or maybe she treats me the same way she treats other friends? Am I special to her or not? Oh God, I almost become crazy whenever I start to think about it.

If she doesn't like me, then why does she talk with me more than other guys? Why does she reply to my text every time even if she's too busy?

By the way, I've learned my lesson, so I'm not going to repeat the same sad story. Last time, I fell in love with my friend who later became a stranger. The experience that I got from her was very depressing.

Now I don't want to be in the same situation, and this is a much more serious problem. I could lose anyone else, but not this friend because she is very important to me, and I never want to lose her from my life. I consider her my precious person, and, indeed, she is.

Still, I should never ever cross the line, or she would leave me.

Who is she?

(**Note:** *Who is she = He is shoe.*)

94

To Deny
You Can't

The beauty of love is very similar to the sunrise. It's glamorous. However, it lasts only for a short period of time. If you fail to notice it, then you might not know what it means to be in love. You might think that it is a common thing to fall in love. In fact, it takes so much to love. The decision. The commitment. The belief. One couldn't truly love if she is unsure about herself. On top of that, when she has even a slightly small doubt, it would ruin everything between her and the guy she loves. She also convinces herself that they both would end up in a bad relationship. She could destroy everything if she keeps thinking that way. We all can accept or reject love, but we can't avoid it because love is the nature of human beings. When you run away from love, it means you are running away from your own life. Can you run away from it? You can't, so stop denying nature. You should embrace it instead of trying to deny it.

95

To Reveal

Who Are You?

I have you in my mind, but I shall never wish for more. Nor do I want to.

I want everything good for you, but it's better if I stay away from you. I will only steal happiness from you if I am with you. In the end, I would destroy your soul and break your heart piece by piece.

You just need to know that I have you in my heart, and I will keep you there for eternity. As long as my soul remains in existence, you will be with me.

Because you are different, I can't risk killing your happiness even if it means I have to endure the thirst and the call for love. I will never ever break your heart because I love you, but I can't be with you.

Anyway, the truth shall remain unchanged, and one day, you shall know that. It shall stand and wait to be unfolded. It shall be there waiting for you. Maybe you would miss it. Maybe you could neglect it, but the truth is there, and it never changes, no matter what. It doesn't matter how long you could avoid seeing it, but the truth is the truth, and nobody can change it. Not even me, even though I wanted to.

The truth that I have always loved you. The truth that you are different from others. The truth that I keep you in my heart forever. The truth that you are the most important person to me. And the truth that we can't be together. Period!

Be that as it may, I shall not reveal the truth just yet.
Who are you?

96

To Tell

Who Is He?

I love someone, but I don't want him to know about that. Clearly, I never want him to love me back either.

It's not that I'm afraid that he won't love me back. It's because I only want to love him, but I don't want to expect anything in return.

I want to create a beautiful memory only I can see, and I alone can have.

I have come to a point where love between a girl and a guy is so fragile. I tried to protect it but failed. It hurt a lot. Now I don't want to be hurt again.

I just want to have someone in my heart, and I can think about him whenever I need someone to cheer me up.

I want someone with whom I can share my stories. I want someone who can ask me about my day and how I feel. I want someone who will stay by my side. I want someone who can tell me that I am awesome even though I am not.

I want that someone to be my forever someone. Can I have someone like that? However, I don't want to be his someone. I don't want him to think of me as a girlfriend because, one day, I may hurt him.

Maybe I am selfish, but that's all I ever want, and I want him to understand that. I want him to know that I will be there for him when he needs me. I will always believe and support him.

I want him to live his life again because he has tortured himself for too long, due to some mistakes he had made in the past. I want him to know that we make mistakes, from time to time, because we are human beings. The most important thing is that we can learn from our mistakes and correct ourselves.

I want him to really understand this simple truth.

By the way, I shouldn't tell him the truth about my feelings for him. Who is he?

(**Note:** *Who is he = He is who.*)

97

To Show

Should Not

I am not so certain about your feelings towards me, but I am very sure that I am in love with you despite the fact that we just know each other.

We are from different generations, and you are too young to love an old person like me. Plus, you are so amazing that it's impossible for me to be with you. Still, I have fallen in love with you even though there is no hope. To you, I'm just another friend.

You may not prefer to love the type of person like me because I'm old-fashioned, and I'm also a boring person. Maybe we both are from different worlds. My world is ugly, and yours is way more beautiful.

I should not show you my ugly world.

98

To Reject
My Life

The present might be able to take you away from me, but it can't take away the good things that we had together in the past. There's nothing in this world that can change the past that we had and created.

The difference is that I make peace with my past, so I won't have to scare myself again. I won't have to worry about losing you because you are in my mind forever. I just need to keep you in a secret place so that nobody could find you.

In the past, I thought it was a bad idea to keep you in my mind. Now I'm sure that you are in my heart, so I just have to learn to accept you peacefully.

I was blinded by the thought of evil and attempted to erase you from my mind without knowing what was right or wrong. I neglected the truth and tried foolishly to bury it with my own mistakes. Now I realize that I had been so wrong and so foolish. How can I unlearn the very thing that brings meaning to my life?

I simply fail to understand that simple truth. In fact, I should be grateful. You've brought meaning to my life once again. You've changed me, and you've made me a better person.

I want you to know that you have saved my life. You have brought the gift to me, and that gift is never going anywhere from me again.

Thank you for bringing my life back.

IMPOSSIBLE CRUSH

I shouldn't reject my own life.

99

To Answer

Do You Know?

I am in love with your eyes. They are so beautiful, and I couldn't stop thinking about you.

You are very cute and adorable. I have to admit that I am in love with your cuteness also.

I know we are destined to meet, and I also know you come into my life for a purpose. I mean, you have been brought to me by divine guidance, and I can't deny it even if I want to. You come to show me that I finally met the right person. You come into my life to stay, not leave like others. I know you will stay by my side and support me.

You are a good person. I am very lucky to have met a person like you. I am grateful and happy to be a part of your life journey too. Thank you so much.

Do you know who you are? I won't answer this for you.

100

To Break

I Won't Break Your Heart

My eyes are on the computer, but my mind is always busy thinking about you. I always check my phone to see if you have replied to my chat or not.

Having a conversation with you is the happiest thing for me. I even smile alone when I think about it again and again.

You are a gift sent to me by God to brighten my world, and my life starts to have a meaning once again because of you. You have shown me a better chance to really live a better life, unlike the one I lived before. You have come to show me and empower me to be strong and hopeful. I won't let you down. I will never ever screw up this relationship if you ever give me the chance. I promise to protect your heart. I love you.

I won't break your heart.

Thank God!